I0429992

The Startup Strategist
A Blueprint for Entrepreneurial Success

RAYMOND M PENNY

Copyright © 2024
Raymond M Penny
All rights reserved.
ISBN: 9798883764416

TABLE OF CONTENT

Prologue:
A Journey into the Heart of Entrepreneurship

In the vast landscape of business and innovation, entrepreneurship stands as a beacon of bold aspirations, untamed creativity, and unyielding determination. It is a realm where visionaries, risk-takers, and changemakers converge, driven by an insatiable hunger to leave an indelible mark on the world.

Our journey into the heart of entrepreneurship is punctuated by the stories of fearless individuals who have defied convention, shattered barriers, and carved their own paths in pursuit of their dreams. It is a journey that transcends the confines of traditional business models, embracing the boundless spirit of innovation, resilience, and unwavering passion.

Throughout the chapters of this book, we embark on a transformative odyssey, weaving through the intricacies of entrepreneurship – from the inception of a groundbreaking idea to the intricate tapestry of strategic planning, from the exhilarating highs of success to the humbling lessons found within the depths of failure. Each chapter unfolds a new dimension of the entrepreneurial landscape, offering profound insights, actionable strategies, and invaluable wisdom garnered from the experiences of seasoned entrepreneurs and industry experts.

As we delve into the diverse facets of entrepreneurship, we unravel the essence of self-reflection, identifying passion and expertise, understanding market trends, crafting robust business plans, navigating legal complexities, harnessing the power of digital marketing, and so much more. Our exploration transcends the mere mechanics of business; it delves into the very core of what it means to be an entrepreneur – to innovate, adapt, and inspire change.

The protagonists in our narrative are the men and women who embody the spirit of tenacity, resilience, and audacious creativity. Their stories serve as a poignant reminder that entrepreneurship is not merely about creating businesses; it is about igniting transformative movements, fostering meaningful change, and forging a legacy that extends far beyond the realms of commerce.

Join me as we venture into the heart of entrepreneurship, where every challenge is an opportunity, every setback a lesson, and every success an affirmation of our unwavering commitment to innovation and progress. Together, let us illuminate the path for those who dare to dream, inspire those who seek guidance, and celebrate the unbreakable spirit of entrepreneurs around the world.

We begin this extraordinary expedition with open hearts, curious minds, and unyielding determination, embracing the boundless potential that lies within the realm of entrepreneurship. Welcome to the transformative journey of "The Startup Strategist: A Blueprint for Entrepreneurial Success."

May this prologue set the stage for an enlightening and empowering exploration of entrepreneurship. If you have specific themes or aspects you'd like to emphasize, please feel free to share, and I will be delighted to tailor the narrative to your preferences.

DEDICATION

To Every Courageous Entrepreneur

As an entrepreneur myself, I understand firsthand the challenges, uncertainties, and unwavering determination that define the entrepreneurial journey. This book is dedicated to each and every individual who has dared to dream, who has taken the bold steps to transform their vision into reality, and who has embraced the exhilarating yet arduous path of entrepreneurship.

Your resilience, creativity, and unyielding spirit in the face of adversity inspire me and countless others. This dedication is a tribute to your unwavering perseverance, relentless pursuit of innovation, and commitment to making a meaningful impact through the entrepreneurial endeavors you embark upon.

May this book serve as a guiding light, offering insights, wisdom, and practical strategies to support you on your entrepreneurial odyssey. It is my sincere hope that within these pages, you'll find the inspiration, knowledge, and encouragement to navigate the challenges, seize the opportunities, and ultimately, achieve the success you envision.

Here's to the trailblazers, the risk-takers, and the game-changers – those who have taken the courageous leap to make a difference through entrepreneurship. Your passion and dedication illuminate the path for others, and I am honored to dedicate this book to you.

With boundless admiration and unwavering support,
Raymond Penny

INTRODUCTION

Introduction to "The Startup Strategist: A Blueprint for Entrepreneurial Success":

Welcome to "The Startup Strategist: A Blueprint for Entrepreneurial Success," a comprehensive guide designed to equip aspiring entrepreneurs and business professionals with the knowledge, tools, and strategies necessary to thrive in the dynamic world of startups. In this transformative journey through the realms of entrepreneurship, we will explore the essential building blocks that form the foundation of a successful startup venture.

Entrepreneurship is not merely about starting a business; it embodies the spirit of innovation, resilience, and vision. As we delve into the diverse facets of entrepreneurship, from ideation to scaling, this book seeks to empower you with the insights and expertise needed to navigate the challenges and capitalize on the opportunities that define the entrepreneurial landscape.

The book is structured to provide a holistic understanding of the multifaceted aspects of entrepreneurship, covering topics such as self-reflection, identifying passion and expertise, market trends, business planning, financial management, legal considerations, talent acquisition, branding, marketing, networking, innovation, work-life balance, leadership, raising capital, and much more. Each chapter offers actionable advice, real-world examples, and practical strategies to help you embark on your entrepreneurial journey with confidence and clarity.

Drawing from the experiences of seasoned entrepreneurs and industry experts, the book also delves into the nuances of leadership, ethical decision-making, social responsibility, and overcoming common startup challenges. Moreover, it offers valuable insights on embracing innovation, leveraging technology, and adopting a data-driven approach to decision-making in the ever-evolving business environment.

Whether you are a budding entrepreneur with a game-changing idea or a seasoned professional seeking to adapt and grow in the entrepreneurial space, "The Startup Strategist" aims to be your trusted companion, providing invaluable guidance and inspiration along the way.

As we embark on this enlightening expedition, let us explore the intricacies of entrepreneurship, embrace the spirit of fearless innovation, and uncover the secrets to building resilient, adaptable, and impactful startup ventures. Together, let us chart a path towards entrepreneurial success, learning from the wisdom of those who have braved the journey before us and reflecting on the invaluable lessons gleaned from their experiences.

Join me as we unravel the art, science, and heart of entrepreneurship, celebrating the spirit of creativity, determination, and unwavering passion that fuels the extraordinary visionaries and game-changers shaping the future of business.

I hope this introduction captures the essence of the book and sets the stage for an insightful and empowering journey through the world of entrepreneurship. If you need further refinement or have specific preferences, feel free to let me know, and I'll be more than happy to assist!

CHAPTER 1
What is Entrepreneurship?

Entrepreneurship is the process of creating or starting a new business or venture, often with a focus on innovation, growth, and profitability. Entrepreneurs are individuals who take on the risk and responsibility of starting and running a business, often with a vision to create something new or disrupt an existing market.

At its core, entrepreneurship is about identifying opportunities and turning them into viable businesses. This involves a range of skills and activities, including market research, product development, financing, marketing, and management.

Entrepreneurship can take many forms, from small businesses and startups to social enterprises and scalable ventures. It can also involve different types of entrepreneurships, such as:

* Social entrepreneurship, which aims to create positive social impact alongside financial returns
* Technological entrepreneurship, which focuses on developing and commercializing new technologies
* E-commerce entrepreneurship, which involves building and growing online businesses

In this book, we will explore the concepts, skills, and strategies necessary to succeed as an entrepreneur. We will delve into the entrepreneurial mindset, the process of developing and validating business ideas, and the various paths to raising capital and building a successful venture.

Whether you're a seasoned entrepreneur or just starting out, this book aims to provide you with the knowledge and insights to turn your vision into a successful business.

CHAPTER 2
The Entrepreneurial Mindset

The entrepreneurial mindset is a way of thinking and approaching problems that is essential for success in today's fast-paced and ever-changing business landscape. It is characterized by a willingness to take risks, a passion for learning, and a focus on creating value for others.

At its core, the entrepreneurial mindset is about being curious, creative, and resilient. It involves seeing opportunities where others see challenges and taking calculated risks to bring those opportunities to life. It also involves being adaptable and responsive to change and being open to learning from failure.

One of the key characteristics of the entrepreneurial mindset is a willingness to experiment and try new things. This involves being comfortable with uncertainty and taking calculated risks to test new ideas and assumptions. It also involves being open to feedback and willing to pivot or adjust courses as needed.

Another important aspect of the entrepreneurial mindset is a focus on creating value for others. This involves understanding the needs and pain points of customers and working to create solutions that meet those needs. It also involves being customer-centric and empathetic, and constantly seeking feedback and insights from customers.

Developing an entrepreneurial mindset can benefit individuals and organizations in many ways. It can lead to increased creativity and innovation, improved problem-solving skills, and a greater willingness to take calculated risks. It can also lead to greater resilience and adaptability in the face of change and uncertainty.

So how can you develop an entrepreneurial mindset? Here are a few practical strategies:

*   Embrace lifelong learning and seek out new experiences and knowledge
*   Take calculated risks and embrace uncertainty
*   Focus on creating value for others and understand their needs and pain points
*   Be adaptable and resilient in the face of change and setbacks
*   Surround yourself with diverse perspectives and collaborate with others
*   Practice self-awareness and reflection to continually improve and grow

By adopting an entrepreneurial mindset, individuals and organizations can unlock their full potential and achieve greater success and impact in today's dynamic and uncertain world.

CHAPTER 3

Self-Reflection: Are You Ready to Become an entrepreneur?

Idea generation is the process of creating and identifying potential business ideas. Opportunity recognition involves spotting viable opportunities that align with your passions, skills, and resources. Effective idea generation and opportunity recognition require a combination of creativity, curiosity, and analysis.

Sources of Ideas

Ideas can come from a variety of sources, including:

1. Personal experiences and observations
2. Customer feedback and pain points
3. Industry trends and emerging markets
4. New technologies and innovations
5. Competitor analysis
6. Brainstorming and ideation techniques

Idea Filtering and Refining

Once you have a list of potential ideas, it's important to filter and refine them to identify the most promising opportunities. This involves:

1. Conducting market research and analysis
2. Assessing the competition and market gap

3.   Evaluating the feasibility and scalability of the idea
4.   Aligning the idea with your passions, skills, and resources
5.   Refining the idea based on feedback and iteration

Opportunity Recognition

Opportunity recognition involves identifying potential opportunities that align with your skills, resources, and interests. This involves:

1.   Identifying unmet needs or pain points in the market
2.   Recognizing emerging trends and technologies
3.   Analyzing customer behavior and preferences
4.   Spotting weaknesses or gaps in the competition
5.   Leveraging your unique strengths and expertise

Idea generation and opportunity recognition are critical steps in the entrepreneurial journey. By combining creativity, curiosity, and analysis, entrepreneurs can identify promising ideas and opportunities that align with their passions and resources. Remember, the most successful businesses often start with a great idea that meets a real need in the market.

CHAPTER 4
Identifying Your Passion and Expertise

As an entrepreneur, your passion and expertise are the foundation upon which you will build your business. Your passion provides the drive and motivation to pursue your ideas, while your expertise gives you the credibility and skills to execute them.

Understanding Your Passion

Your passion is the fuel that drives you to take risks, push boundaries, and persevere through challenges. To identify your passion, ask yourself:

What sparks your enthusiasm and excitement?

What activities do you enjoy and find most engaging?

What values and beliefs are most important to you?

What experiences have you had that have brought you the greatest sense of fulfillment and satisfaction?

Understanding Your Expertise

Your expertise is the specialized knowledge and skills that set you apart and enable you to create value in the market. To identify your expertise, consider:

What skills have you developed over the years through education, training, and experience?

What are your natural talents and strengths?

What areas have you received recognition or feedback for your skills and abilities?

What unique insights or perspectives do you bring to your industry or field?

The Intersection of Passion and Expertise

The sweet spot for entrepreneurial success lies at the intersection of your passion and expertise. When you combine what you love with what you're good at, you'll find:

Increased motivation and engagement

Authenticity and confidence

A unique value proposition.

A competitive advantage

Greater fulfillment and purpose

Developing Your Passion and Expertise

To further develop your passion and expertise, try:

Experimenting with different areas to discover what resonates with you.

Seeking feedback from others to gain new insights and perspectives.

Continuously learning and upskilling to stay current and competitive.

Reflecting on your experiences and progress to identify areas for growth.

Embracing your uniqueness and strengths to stand out in your industry.

By understanding and embracing your passion and expertise, you'll be well on your way to building a successful and fulfilling entrepreneurial career.

CHAPTER 5
Defining Your Business Model

Your business model is the blueprint for how you will create and deliver value to your customers, and how you will generate revenue and grow your business. Defining your business model requires consideration of several key components, including:

Customer Segments

Who are your target customers? What are their needs, wants, and pain points? How will you segment and target specific groups?

Value Proposition

What unique value do you offer to your customers? What problem do you solve, and how do you solve it? What sets you apart from competitors?

Channels

How will you reach and engage with your customers? What channels will you use to market, sell, and deliver your product or service?

Customer Relationships

What kind of relationship do you want to have with your customers? How will you build and maintain those relationships?

Revenue Streams

How will you generate revenue? What pricing strategy will you use? What are the potential revenue streams for your business?

Key Resources

What resources do you need to execute your business model? What are the essential assets, skills, and expertise required?

Key Activities

What activities are essential to your business model? What are the main operational processes and tasks required?

Key Partnerships

What partnerships are critical to your success? What collaborations or alliances will you form to achieve your goals?

Once you have a clear understanding of these components, you can begin to design and refine your business model. This may involve experimenting with different channels, pricing strategies, or revenue streams to find the right fit for your business.

Remember, your business model is not a static document – it is a dynamic and evolving framework that will be needed to adapt to changing market conditions and customer needs. By regularly reviewing and refining your business model, you can ensure that your business remains competitive, innovative, and aligned with your vision and goals.

CHAPTER 6
Building Your Business Plan

Now that you have a solid understanding of your business model, it's time to build a comprehensive business plan. Your business plan is a detailed roadmap that outlines your goals, strategies, and tactics for launching and growing your business.

Executive Summary

Your executive summary is a brief overview of your business, including your mission statement, products or services, target market, and financial goals. This section should entice readers to want to learn more about your business.

Company Description

This section provides a more detailed overview of your business, including its history, structure, and ownership. You'll also outline your business's values, vision, and mission statement.

Market Analysis

In this section, you'll conduct a thorough analysis of your industry, competitors, and target market. You'll identify market trends, opportunities, and challenges, and explain how your business will differentiate itself from the competition.

Organization & Management

Here, you'll outline the legal structure of your business, its organizational chart, and the responsibilities of each team member.

You'll also discuss your human resources plan, including staffing, training, and employee development.

Marketing & Sales

This section details your marketing and sales strategies, including your branding, advertising, promotions, and pricing tactics. You'll also outline your sales process, including lead generation, conversion rates, and customer retention strategies.

Service or Product Line

In this section, you'll describe your products or services in detail, including their features, benefits, and how they meet the needs of your target market.

Financial Projections

This section contains your financial projections, including income statements, balance sheets, and cash flow statements. You'll also outline your funding requirements, assumptions, and risk factors.

Finally, you'll include any additional information that supports your business plan, such as market research, product specifications, or legal documents.

By completing a comprehensive business plan, you'll have a clear and actionable roadmap for launching and growing your business. Remember to review and update your plan regularly to ensure you stay on track and adapt to changing market conditions.

CHAPTER 7

Building Your Brand

Your brand is the identity, image, and personality of your business. It's what sets you apart from competitors and makes you memorable to customers. Building a strong brand requires careful consideration of several key elements, including:

Brand Positioning

This refers to the unique space your brand occupies in the market. You'll need to identify your target audience, their needs and wants, and how your brand meets those needs.

Brand Personality

This is the character and tone of your brand. Are you fun and playful, or serious and professional? Consistency is key to building a strong brand personality.

Brand Messaging

This is the language and tone you use to communicate with your audience. Your messaging should be clear, concise, and consistent across all channels.

Visual Identity

This includes your logo, color palette, typography, and imagery. Your visual identity should be distinctive, memorable, and scalable.

Voice and Tone

This is the way you communicate with your audience through written and spoken words. Your voice and tone should be consistent and aligned with your brand personality.

Brand Guidelines

These are the rules and standards that govern how your brand is represented. Consistency is key to building a strong brand, so it's important to have guidelines in place.

Brand Storytelling

This is the art of sharing your brand's history, values, and mission through compelling narratives. Storytelling helps create an emotional connection with your audience.

Brand Engagement

This is the process of interacting with your audience and building relationships. Engagement can happen through social media, customer service, and other touchpoints.

By building a strong brand, you'll establish trust and credibility with your audience, differentiate yourself from competitors, and create a lasting impression in the market. Remember, your brand is a living, breathing entity that evolves with your business, so continuous attention and nurturing are essential.

CHAPTER 8

Building Your Online Presence

In today's digital age, having a strong online presence is crucial for businesses. Your website, social media, and other online platforms are often the first impression potential customers have of your brand. Building a robust online presence requires consideration of several key elements, including:

Website Design

Your website is often the hub of your online presence. It should be visually appealing, easy to navigate, and optimized for search engines.

Content Creation

High-quality, engaging content is essential for attracting and retaining a clearly defined audience. This includes blog posts, videos, social media posts, and more.

Search Engine Optimization (SEO)

SEO involves optimizing your website and online content to rank higher in search engine results pages. This includes keyword research, on-page optimization, and link building.

Social Media Marketing

Social media platforms like Facebook, Instagram, and Twitter are powerful tools for engaging with customers and promoting your brand.

Email Marketing

Building an email list and sending regular newsletters is an effective way to nurture leads and stay top of mind with customers.

Online Advertising

Paid advertising on platforms like Google AdWords, Facebook Ads, and LinkedIn Ads can help drive traffic and generate leads.

Influencer Marketing

Partnering with influencers in your industry can help expand your reach and build credibility with their followers.

Analytics and Reporting

Tracking your online performance using tools like Google Analytics and social media insights helps you measure success and make data-driven decisions.

By building a strong online presence, you'll increase your visibility, engagement, and conversion rates, ultimately driving business growth. Remember, your online presence is an ongoing effort that requires regular updates and optimization to stay ahead of the competition.

CHAPTER 9

Building Your Team

As your business grows, you'll need to assemble a team of talented and dedicated professionals to help you achieve your goals. Building a strong team requires careful consideration of several key elements, including:

Defining Your Team's Roles and Responsibilities

Clearly define each team member's role, responsibilities, and expectations to avoid confusion and ensure everyone is working towards the same objectives.

Recruiting and Hiring

Attract, select, and hire the best candidates for each role, considering skills, experience, culture fit, and potential for growth.

Onboarding and Training

Develop a comprehensive onboarding program that introduces new team members to your business, culture, and processes, and provides ongoing training and development opportunities.

Team Building and Culture

Foster a positive, inclusive, and supportive team culture that encourages collaboration, innovation, and creativity.

Performance Management

Establish regular check-ins, feedback, and performance evaluations to ensure team members are meeting expectations and growing professionally.

Employee Engagement and Retention

Prioritize employee satisfaction and retention by offering competitive compensation, benefits, and perks, and creating a positive work environment.

Leadership and Management

Develop strong leadership and management skills to motivate, guide, and support your team, and empower them to take ownership and make decisions.

By building a talented and cohesive team, you'll unlock the potential for growth, innovation, and success in your business. Remember, your team is your greatest asset, and investing in their development and well-being is essential for long-term prosperity.

CHAPTER 10

Scaling Your Business

You've built a solid foundation, and now it's time to take your business to the next level. Scaling your business requires careful planning, strategic decision-making, and a willingness to adapt. In this chapter, we'll explore various strategies to help you grow your business sustainably and efficiently.

Assessing Readiness to Scale

Before scaling, evaluate your business's readiness. Consider factors like financial stability, market demand, operational efficiency, talent acquisition and retention, and technological infrastructure.

Identifying Growth Opportunities

Analyze your market, industry trends, and customer needs to identify growth opportunities. Consider expanding product lines or services, entering new markets or geographies, partnerships and collaborations, and diversifying revenue streams.

Scaling Strategies

Choose the best scaling strategies for your business, such as horizontal scaling (expanding existing products/services), vertical scaling (deepening existing products/services), platform scaling (creating a platform for others to build on), and service-based scaling (offering services complementary to your product).

Building a Scalable Business Model

Develop a scalable business model by standardizing processes, automating tasks, outsourcing non-core functions, and developing a robust technology infrastructure.

Leveraging Technology for Growth

Harness technology to streamline operations, enhance customer experience, and drive growth through data analytics and visualization, cloud computing and infrastructure, marketing automation and CRM, and e-commerce and digital channels.

Measuring and Managing Growth

Track key performance indicators (KPIs) to measure growth and make data-driven decisions. Focus on revenue growth, customer acquisition and retention, operational efficiency, and cash flow management.

Scaling Your Team and Culture

As you grow, scale your team and culture by developing a strong leadership pipeline, fostering a culture of innovation and experimentation, investing in employee development and engagement, and building diverse and inclusive teams.

Remember, scaling your business is a journey, not a destination. Stay agile, adapt to changing circumstances, and remain focused on your vision to achieve long-term success.

CHAPTER 11

Building Strong Partnerships

As your business grows, you'll come to realize that you can't do everything alone. Building strong partnerships with suppliers, vendors, collaborators, and even competitors can help you achieve your goals more efficiently. In this chapter, we'll explore the art of building and maintaining partnerships that benefit both parties.

Identifying Potential Partners

To build strong partnerships, you must first identify potential partners who can help you achieve your objectives. Ask yourself who shares your values and vision, who can complement your strengths and weaknesses, and who can help you reach new heights.

Building Relationships

Building strong relationships with partners requires effort and dedication. Communication is key - listening actively and share openly. Trust is also essential - be transparent and reliable. Shared goals are equally important - align your objectives and expectations. And finally, mutual respect is vital - value each other's expertise and opinions.

Partnership Agreements

To formalize partnerships, create agreements that outline key terms such as roles and responsibilities, expectations and goals, confidentiality and IP protection, and dispute resolution and termination clauses.

Collaborative Problem-Solving

Embrace collaborative problem-solving by sharing knowledge and expertise, identifying and addressing potential issues, and jointly developing solutions and contingency plans.

Conflict Resolution

Develop a process for resolving conflicts constructively by communicating openly and honestly, focusing on interests, not positions, and seeking mediation or arbitration when needed.

Maintaining Partnerships

Nurture partnerships over time by regular communication and feedback, adapting to changing needs and circumstances, and showing appreciation and recognition.

By building and maintaining strong partnerships, you'll gain access to new resources, expertise, and networks, ultimately driving growth and success for all parties involved.

CHAPTER 12

Funding Your Business: Bootstrapping vs. Seeking Investors

As an entrepreneur, securing funding is a critical step in transforming your business idea into a successful venture. You are faced with two primary options: bootstrapping or seeking investors. In this chapter, we will delve into the advantages and disadvantages of each approach, empowering you to make an informed decision that aligns with your business vision and personal preferences.

Bootstrapping: Financing Your Dream

Bootstrapping involves utilizing your own savings, revenue from early customers, and cost-cutting strategies to fund your business. This approach allows you to maintain control and avoid accumulating debt. With bootstrapping, you retain ownership and enjoy faster decision-making, but growth may be slower, and resources may be limited.

Seeking Investors: Partnering for Growth

Seeking investors involves presenting your business to potential investors, such as angel investors, venture capitalists, or crowdfunding platforms. This path provides access to capital, networking opportunities, and expert guidance. However, you must consider the trade-offs: sharing ownership and control, and managing high expectations for returns.

Choosing Your Path

When deciding between bootstrapping and seeking investors, reflect on your business stage, growth aspirations, and personal comfort level with ownership dilution. Consider how much funding you require, your growth projections, and your willingness to share control. By carefully evaluating these factors, you can select the approach that harmonizes with your entrepreneurial vision.

Remember, funding is merely one aspect of your journey. Success demands dedication, adaptability, and wise decision-making. Embrace the path that aligns with your business and personal values, and continue to nurture your venture towards long-term prosperity.

CHAPTER 13
Managing Financial Risks

As an entrepreneur, managing financial risks is crucial to ensure the stability and growth of your business. In this chapter, we will explore various financial risks and strategies to mitigate them, helping you protect your venture and achieve long-term success.

Understanding Financial Risks

Financial risks can arise from various sources, including market fluctuations, customer payments, supplier agreements, and economic changes. These risks can impact your cash flow, profitability, and overall financial health. Common financial risks include:

Market risk: changes in market conditions affecting your investments or assets

Credit risk: customers defaulting on payments

Liquidity risk: difficulty meeting short-term financial obligations

Operational risk: inefficient processes or system failures

Currency risk: changes in exchange rates impacting international transactions

Mitigating Financial Risks

To manage financial risks effectively, consider the following strategies:

Diversification: spread investments and revenue streams to minimize market risk

Credit checks and contracts: assess customer creditworthiness and establish clear payment terms

Cash reserve: maintain a safety net for unexpected expenses or revenue shortfalls

Risk assessment: regularly review processes and systems to identify and address vulnerabilities

Hedging: use financial instruments to manage currency or market risks

By understanding and addressing financial risks, you can safeguard your business and ensure its continued growth and profitability. Remember, risk management is an ongoing process that requires regular monitoring and adaptation to changing circumstances.

CHAPTER 14

Understanding Legal and Regulatory Requirements

As an entrepreneur, navigating the legal and regulatory landscape is essential to avoid pitfalls and ensure your business's compliance and success. In this chapter, we will explore various legal and regulatory requirements, providing you with a solid understanding of the frameworks that govern business operations.

Legal Structures: Forming Your Business

Choosing the right legal structure is a critical decision, as it affects taxation, liability, and ownership. Common legal structures include:

Sole proprietorship: simplest form, personal liability

Partnership: shared ownership, shared liability

Limited liability company (LLC): hybrid, combines liability protection with tax benefits

Corporation: separate legal entity, shareholder ownership

Regulatory Requirements: Compliance and Licensing

Depending on your industry, location, and activities, your business may need to comply with various regulations and obtain licenses or permits. Familiarize yourself with requirements related to:

Employment and labor laws

Data privacy and security regulations

Environmental regulations

Zoning and land use requirements

Intellectual property protection (patents, trademarks, copyrights)

Staying Informed and Compliant

Stay up-to-date with changes in legal and regulatory requirements by:

Monitoring government agency websites and news

Consulting with legal counsel or regulatory experts

Participating in industry associations and advocacy groups

Conducting regular compliance audits and risk assessments

By understanding and adhering to legal and regulatory requirements, you can protect your business from legal disputes, fines, and reputational damage. Remember, compliance is an ongoing process that demands continuous attention and vigilance.

CHAPTER 15

Finding and Retaining the Right Talent

Attracting and retaining top talent is the cornerstone of building a successful organization. In today's competitive job market, it's essential to have a comprehensive strategy in place to find and keep the best employees.

Defining Your Requirements

Before beginning your search, it's important to clearly define the skills, qualifications, and qualities you need in a candidate. Consider the specific tasks and responsibilities of the role, as well as the team's dynamics and company culture.

Utilizing Recruitment Channels

Post job ads on social media, job boards, and your website to reach a wide audience. Consider partnering with recruitment agencies or leveraging employee referrals to find top talent.

Emphasizing Company Culture

Highlight your company culture, values, and mission to attract candidates who align with your vision. Showcase your work environment, company benefits, and growth opportunities to appeal to top talent.

Offering Competitive Compensation

Provide salaries and benefits that are competitive with industry standards to attract and retain top performers. Consider offering flexible work arrangements, professional development opportunities, and recognition programs to sweeten the deal.

Developing a Strong Onboarding Process

Ensure new hires feel welcome and prepared for their role with a comprehensive onboarding program. Provide clear expectations, job training, and mentorship to set them up for success.

Fostering Growth and Development

Encourage continuous learning and growth opportunities to retain top performers. Offer training programs, mentorship, and career advancement opportunities to keep them engaged and motivated.

Regularly Evaluating and Improving

Continuously assess your recruitment and retention strategies to ensure they are effective. Gather feedback from employees and make necessary adjustments to stay competitive in the job market.

By implementing these strategies, you can find and retain the right talent to drive your business forward. Remember, attracting and retaining top performers is an ongoing process that requires regular attention and improvement.

CHAPTER 16

Creating a Compelling Brand Identity

A strong brand identity is essential for any business to stand out in today's crowded marketplace. Your brand identity is the sum total of how your business is perceived by your customers, and it's what sets you apart from your competitors. In this chapter, we'll explore the key elements of a compelling brand identity and how to create one that resonates with your target audience.

Defining Your Brand

Start by defining your brand's mission, values, and personality. What problem do you solve for your customers? What sets your business apart? What values do you want to convey to your audience?

Visual Identity

Your visual identity includes your logo, color palette, typography, and imagery. These elements should be consistent across all channels and should reflect your brand's personality and values.

Messaging and Positioning

Develop a clear and concise messaging strategy that communicates your brand's unique value proposition. Position your brand in the market by identifying your unique niche and what sets you apart from the competition.

Consistency and Authenticity

Consistency is key to building a strong brand identity. Ensure that your branding is consistent across all channels, including your website, social media, and advertising. Authenticity is also crucial - be true to your brand's values and mission.

Emotional Connection

Create an emotional connection with your audience by sharing your brand's story and values. Use language and imagery that resonates with your target audience and creates a sense of belonging.

Evolution and Adaptation

Brands are not static - they evolve and adapt over time. Continuously monitor your brand's performance and make adjustments as needed to stay relevant and competitive.

By creating a compelling brand identity, you'll build a strong foundation for your business and establish a deep connection with your customers. Remember, your brand identity is how your customers perceive you - make it count!

CHAPTER 17

Developing a Marketing Strategy

A well-crafted marketing strategy is essential to effectively reach and engage with your target audience. In this chapter, we'll explore the key components of a marketing strategy and provide guidance on how to develop and implement a successful plan.

Defining Your Target Audience

Identify your ideal customer by understanding their demographics, psychographics, and pain points. This will help you create messaging that resonates with your audience.

Marketing Objectives

Establish clear and measurable marketing objectives, such as increasing website traffic or boosting sales. This will help you focus your efforts and track progress.

Marketing Mix

Develop a comprehensive marketing mix by leveraging the 4Ps: Product, Price, Promotion, and Place. Consider how each element will contribute to achieving your marketing objectives.

Content Marketing

Create a content marketing strategy that aligns with your target audience's needs and interests. Use various formats like blog posts, videos, and social media to engage and educate your audience.

Measurement and Evaluation

Track and analyze your marketing efforts using key performance indicators (KPIs) such as website analytics, customer feedback, and sales data. Use this information to refine and optimize your marketing strategy.

Budgeting and Resources

Allocate a dedicated budget and resources for your marketing efforts. Ensure that your team has the necessary skills and tools to execute your marketing strategy effectively.

Adapting to Change

Stay agile and responsive to changes in the market, consumer behavior, and technology. Continuously monitor and adjust your marketing strategy to optimize results.

By developing a comprehensive marketing strategy, you'll be equipped to effectively reach, engage, and convert your target audience into loyal customers. Remember, a successful marketing strategy is iterative, so be prepared to adapt and evolve with the changing landscape.

CHAPTER 18

Leveraging Digital Marketing Channels

In today's digital age, leveraging digital marketing channels is crucial for businesses to reach and engage with their target audience. Digital marketing channels offer a range of benefits, including increased reach, precision targeting, and measurable results. In this chapter, we will explore the various digital marketing channels available and provide guidance on how to effectively utilize them to achieve business goals.

Search Engine Optimization (SEO)

Search engine optimization (SEO) is the process of optimizing website content to rank higher in search engine results pages (SERPs). By optimizing for search engines, businesses can increase their visibility in organic search results, driving more traffic to their website.

Pay-Per-Click (PPC) Advertising

Pay-per-click (PPC) advertising is a form of online advertising where businesses pay each time a user clicks on their ad. PPC campaigns can be highly effective for driving targeted traffic to a website, as businesses only pay for ads that are clicked.

Social Media Marketing

Social media marketing involves leveraging social media platforms like Facebook, Twitter, and Instagram to reach and engage with a target audience. Social media marketing can be used for brand awareness, lead generation, and customer engagement.

Email Marketing

Email marketing involves sending targeted and personalized messages to a list of subscribers. Email marketing can be used for lead nurturing, customer engagement, and conversion optimization.

Content Marketing

Content marketing involves creating and distributing valuable, relevant, and consistent content to attract and retain a clearly defined audience. Content marketing can be used for brand awareness, lead generation, and customer engagement.

Mobile Marketing

Mobile marketing involves leveraging mobile devices to reach and engage with a target audience. Mobile marketing can be used for SMS marketing, push notifications, and mobile-optimized advertising.

Video Marketing

Video marketing involves leveraging video content to reach and engage with a target audience. Video marketing can be used for brand awareness, lead generation, and customer engagement.

Influencer Marketing

Influencer marketing involves partnering with influencers who have a large following in your target audience. Influencer marketing can be used for brand awareness, lead generation, and customer engagement.

Podcast Marketing

Podcast marketing involves leveraging podcasts to reach and engage with a target audience. Podcast marketing can be used for brand awareness, lead generation, and customer engagement.

Measuring and Optimizing Digital Marketing Performance

To maximize the effectiveness of digital marketing campaigns, it's essential to measure and optimize performance regularly. This involves tracking key performance indicators (KPIs) such as website traffic, conversion rates, and return on investment (ROI). By regularly analyzing and optimizing digital marketing campaigns, businesses can improve their overall performance and achieve their marketing goals.

In conclusion, leveraging digital marketing channels can help businesses reach and engage with their target audience more effectively. By understanding the various digital marketing channels available and implementing a comprehensive digital marketing strategy, businesses can drive more traffic, generate more leads, and ultimately increase revenue.

CHAPTER 19
Sales Strategies for Startups

As a startup, developing a sales strategy that works for your business is crucial for growth and success. In this chapter, we will explore various sales strategies that startups can leverage to acquire and retain customers.

Understanding Your Target Market

Before developing a sales strategy, it's essential to understand your target market. Who are your ideal customers? What are their pain points? What are their goals and challenges? Knowing your target market inside and out will help you tailor your sales approach to their needs.

Identifying Your Unique Selling Proposition (USP)

Your USP is what sets your product or service apart from the competition. What makes your offering unique? Why should customers choose your product or service over others in the market? Your USP will be the foundation of your sales messaging and strategy.

Building a Sales Funnel

A sales funnel is the process by which a lead becomes a customer. It typically consists of several stages, including awareness, interest, consideration, and conversion. Developing a sales funnel will help you understand where leads are dropping off and how to optimize each stage for higher conversions.

Developing a Sales Process

A sales process is the series of steps your team takes to close a deal. This includes prospecting, qualifying, demonstrating, and closing. Developing a sales process will help your team stay organized and focused on closing deals.

Cultivating Relationships

Building relationships with customers and prospects is crucial for startup success. This includes understanding their needs, providing value, and following up regularly. Relationships will help you retain customers and generate referrals.

Leveraging Technology

Technology can be a powerful tool for startups looking to streamline their sales process. This includes using customer relationship management (CRM) software, sales automation tools, and data analytics to track performance and optimize results.

Measuring and Optimizing Performance

Tracking key performance indicators (KPIs) like conversion rates, sales cycle length, and customer acquisition cost will help you measure the effectiveness of your sales strategy. Use data to optimize your approach and improve results over time.

In conclusion, developing a sales strategy that works for your startup requires understanding your target market, identifying your USP, building a sales funnel, developing a sales process, cultivating relationships, leveraging technology, and measuring and optimizing performance. By following these strategies, startups can acquire and retain customers, driving growth and success

CHAPTER 20

Building a Network of Mentors and Advisors

As an entrepreneur, building a network of mentors and advisors can provide invaluable guidance, support, and expertise to help navigate the challenges of starting and growing a business. In this chapter, we will explore the importance of having a mentor or advisor, how to find and approach potential mentors, and how to build and maintain these relationships.

Why You Need a Mentor or Advisor

A mentor or advisor can offer a fresh perspective, share their experience, and provide valuable insights to help you make informed decisions. They can also introduce you to valuable connections, help you avoid common pitfalls, and provide encouragement and motivation when needed.

Finding and Approaching Potential Mentors

Identify potential mentors or advisors through networking events, industry conferences, or online platforms. Reach out to them with a clear and concise message, highlighting your shared interests and goals. Show enthusiasm and respect for their time and expertise.

Building and Maintaining Relationships

Establish clear expectations and communication channels with your mentor or advisor. Be open and transparent about your challenges and progress. Show appreciation for their guidance and support, and be willing to reciprocate with your own expertise and networks.

Diversifying Your Network

Seek out multiple mentors or advisors with diverse backgrounds and expertise to gain a well-rounded perspective. This will help you navigate various aspects of your business and personal growth.

Mentorship Programs and Resources

Explore formal mentorship programs, such as SCORE, Startup Leadership Program, or local entrepreneurship organizations. Utilize online platforms like LinkedIn or Entrepreneurial communities to connect with potential mentors or advisors.

Conclusion

Building a network of mentors and advisors can significantly enhance your entrepreneurial journey. By seeking guidance from experienced professionals, you can avoid common pitfalls, gain valuable insights, and accelerate your business growth. Remember to approach these relationships with respect, openness, and a willingness to learn and reciprocate.

CHAPTER 21
Navigating the Competitive Landscape

As a startup, understanding the competitive landscape is crucial to differentiate yourself and stay ahead of the competition. In this chapter, we will explore how to conduct a competitive analysis, identify market gaps, and develop a competitive strategy to position your startup for success.

Conducting a Competitive Analysis

Identify your direct and indirect competitors, and analyze their strengths, weaknesses, and strategies. Understand their pricing, marketing, and product strategies, and assess their market share and customer base.

Identifying Market Gaps

Look for gaps in the market that your competitors are not addressing. Identify unmet customer needs or opportunities to innovate and disrupt the status quo.

Developing a Competitive Strategy

Based on your analysis, develop a competitive strategy that highlights your unique value proposition, differentiators, and competitive advantages. Position your startup as a leader in your niche or market segment.

Staying Ahead of the Competition

Continuously monitor your competitors and adjust your strategy accordingly. Stay agile and innovative, and focus on delivering exceptional customer value to stay ahead of the competition.

By understanding the competitive landscape and developing a solid competitive strategy, you can position your startup for success and achieve your business goals.

CHAPTER 22

Embracing Innovation and Adaptation

In today's fast-paced business landscape, innovation and adaptation are crucial for staying ahead of the curve. In this chapter, we will explore the importance of embracing innovation and adaptation, how to foster a culture of innovation, and strategies for adapting to change.

The Importance of Innovation and Adaptation

Innovation and adaptation are key drivers of growth and success in business. Companies that embrace innovation and adaptation are better equipped to stay ahead of the competition, meet changing customer needs, and capitalize on new opportunities.

Fostering a Culture of Innovation

To foster a culture of innovation, companies should encourage experimentation, provide resources and support for innovative ideas, and create a safe and inclusive environment where employees feel comfortable sharing their ideas.

Strategies for Adapting to Change

Companies should stay agile and adapt to change by continuously monitoring industry trends, embracing new technologies, and being open to new business models. They should also prioritize continuous learning and professional development for their employees.

Conclusion

In conclusion, innovation and adaptation are essential for business success in today's fast-paced landscape. By fostering a culture of innovation and adopting strategies for adapting to change, companies can stay ahead of the curve and achieve long-term growth and success.

CHAPTER 23

Balancing Work and Personal Life as an Entrepreneur

As an entrepreneur, it can be challenging to strike a balance between work and personal life. However, it is essential to maintain a healthy balance to avoid burnout and ensure long-term success. In this chapter, we will explore the importance of work-life balance, strategies for achieving balance, and tips for maintaining a healthy balance.

Importance of Work-Life Balance

Work-life balance is crucial for entrepreneurs as it allows them to recharge, refocus, and maintain a healthy perspective. Without balance, entrepreneurs risk burnout, strained relationships, and decreased productivity.

Strategies for Achieving Balance

Set clear boundaries: Establish a clear distinction between work and personal time.

Prioritize self-care: Make time for activities that nourish your mind, body, and soul.

Schedule personal time: Treat personal time with the same importance as work commitments.

Delegate and outsource: Free up time by delegating tasks to others.

Embrace flexibility: Be flexible and adapt to changing circumstances.

Tips for Maintaining a Healthy Balance

Take breaks: Regularly take short breaks throughout the day.

Use technology wisely: Technology can be both a blessing and a curse; use it to your advantage.

Communicate with loved ones: Openly communicate your work and personal needs with loved ones.

Practice mindfulness: Stay present and focused in the moment.

Conclusion

Achieving work-life balance as an entrepreneur requires intentional effort and commitment. By prioritizing self-care, setting clear boundaries, and delegating tasks, entrepreneurs can maintain a healthy balance between work and personal life, leading to increased productivity, creativity, and overall well-being.

CHAPTER 24

Dealing with Entrepreneurial Stress and Burnout

As an entrepreneur, stress and burnout can be constant companions. The pressure to succeed, the weight of responsibility, and the never-ending demands on your time and energy can take a toll on your mental and physical health. In this chapter, we will explore the signs and symptoms of entrepreneurial stress and burnout, strategies for managing stress, and tips for preventing burnout.

Signs and Symptoms of Entrepreneurial Stress and Burnout

Chronic fatigue and exhaustion

Irritability and mood swings

Difficulty sleeping or insomnia

Physical symptoms like headaches and stomach problems

Loss of motivation and interest in work

Strategies for Managing Stress

Practice self-care: prioritize activities that bring you joy and relaxation

Exercise regularly: physical activity releases endorphins, reducing stress and anxiety

Mindfulness and meditation: calm your mind and focus on the present

Set realistic goals and expectations: break tasks into manageable chunks

Seek support: share your struggles with trusted friends, family, or a mentor

Tips for Preventing Burnout

Take breaks: regular time off to recharge and refocus

Delegate tasks: share responsibilities with others to lighten your load

Prioritize tasks: focus on high-impact activities and eliminate non-essential tasks

Celebrate milestones: acknowledge and celebrate your achievements

Conclusion

Entrepreneurial stress and burnout can be overwhelming, but they can be managed and prevented. By recognizing the signs and symptoms, practicing self-care, and implementing strategies to manage stress, entrepreneurs can maintain their mental and physical well-being. Remember, taking care of yourself is essential to building a successful and sustainable business.

CHAPTER 25

Understanding Intellectual Property Protection

Intellectual property (IP) protection is a vital aspect of entrepreneurship, as it ensures that your unique ideas and creations are safeguarded from unauthorized use. In this chapter, we will delve into the basics of IP protection, explore the different types of IP, and provide guidance on how to protect and enforce your IP rights.

Understanding Intellectual Property

IP refers to creations of the mind, such as inventions, literary and artistic works, and brand names. IP protection grants exclusive rights to creators, allowing them to control how their work is used and prevent others from exploiting it without permission.

Types of Intellectual Property

Patents: protect novel inventions and innovations

Copyrights: protect original literary and artistic works

Trademarks: protect brand names, logos, and slogans

Trade Secrets: protect confidential information and proprietary knowledge

Design Rights: protect the appearance and design of products

How to Protect Your Intellectual Property

Conduct IP audits: identify and document your IP assets

Register your IP: file for patents, trademarks, and copyrights

Use non-disclosure agreements (NDAs): protect confidential information

Implement IP policies: educate employees and partners on IP protection

Monitor and enforce: regularly search for infringements and take action when necessary

Conclusion

IP protection is essential for entrepreneurs to safeguard their innovations and creations. By understanding the different types of IP, registering your IP, and implementing protection measures, you can ensure that your unique ideas and creations remain yours alone. Remember, IP protection is an ongoing process that requires regular monitoring and enforcement to maintain your competitive edge.

CHAPTER 26
Managing Cash Flow Effectively

Cash flow is the lifeblood of any business. It's the amount of money that comes into and goes out of your business, and it's essential to manage it effectively to ensure your business stays healthy and profitable. In this chapter, we'll explore the importance of cash flow management, how to forecast and track your cash flow, and strategies to improve cash flow management.

Why Cash Flow Management is Crucial

Cash flow is the primary indicator of a business's financial health

It affects your ability to pay bills, employees, and suppliers

It impacts your capacity to invest and grow your business

How to Forecast and Track Cash Flow

Create a cash flow statement: outline incoming and outgoing cash flows

Identify cash flow cycles: understand patterns of cash inflows and outflows

Monitor and adjust: regularly review and update your cash flow projections

Strategies to Improve Cash Flow Management

Maintain a cash reserve: set aside funds for unexpected expenses

Optimize accounts receivable and payable: streamline payment processes

Manage inventory: control stock levels to minimize tie-up capital

Consider invoice financing: unlock funds tied up in outstanding invoices

Conclusion

Effective cash flow management is vital to ensure your business stays afloat and achieves long-term success. By forecasting and tracking your cash flow, identifying areas for improvement, and implementing strategies to optimize cash flow, you can maintain a healthy financial foundation and drive growth. Remember, cash flow management is an ongoing process that requires regular attention and adjustments to ensure your business stays on track.

CHAPTER 27

Negotiation Skills for Entrepreneurs

As an entrepreneur, negotiation is a vital skill that can make a significant difference in your business's success. Whether you're negotiating with investors, partners, suppliers, or customers, the ability to negotiate effectively can help you secure better deals, build stronger relationships, and grow your business. In this chapter, we'll explore the art of negotiation, common negotiation styles, and practical tips to enhance your negotiation skills.

Understanding Negotiation

Negotiation is a collaborative process where two or more parties aim to reach a mutually beneficial agreement. It requires effective communication, active listening, and a willingness to compromise. Negotiation is not about winning or losing, but rather finding a solution that satisfies both parties' interests.

Common Negotiation Styles

Competitive Style: assertive and focused on achieving their own goals

Collaborative Style: focus on finding a mutually beneficial solution

Accommodative Style: prioritize relationships and compromise

Avoidant Style: avoid negotiation altogether

Practical Tips to Enhance Negotiation Skills

Prepare thoroughly: research the other party's needs, goals, and limitations

Listen actively: pay attention to the other party's concerns and interests

Be clear and concise: communicate your goals and needs clearly

Focus on interests, not positions: explore underlying needs and desires

Use time to your advantage: take time to think before responding

Conclusion

Negotiation is a crucial skill for entrepreneurs to master. By understanding the negotiation process, recognizing different negotiation styles, and practicing effective negotiation techniques, you can become a more confident and successful negotiator. Remember, negotiation is about finding a mutually beneficial solution, building strong relationships, and growing your business.

CHAPTER 28

Cultivating a Customer-Centric Culture

In today's competitive business landscape, understanding and meeting customer needs is crucial for success. A customer-centric culture prioritizes customer satisfaction, fostering loyalty and driving growth. In this chapter, we'll explore the importance of customer centricity, how to create a customer-centric culture, and strategies for sustaining it.

Why Customer Centricity Matters

- Customer retention and loyalty
- Positive word-of-mouth and referrals
- Competitive advantage and differentiator
- Improved products and services through customer feedback

Creating a Customer-Centric Culture

- Define and communicate a clear customer-centric vision
- Hire and train customer-focused employees
- Encourage customer feedback and respond promptly
- Embed customer insights into decision-making processes
- Recognize and reward customer-centric behavior

Strategies for Sustaining a Customer-Centric Culture

- Regularly collect and analyze customer data
- Empower frontline staff to make customer-centric decisions
- Foster cross-functional collaboration for customer solutions
- Continuously innovate and improve customer experiences
- Lead by example, with customer-centric leadership

Conclusion

A customer-centric culture is vital for businesses seeking long-term success. By understanding customer needs, creating a customer-focused environment, and sustaining this culture, entrepreneurs can build strong relationships, drive growth, and stay ahead of the competition. Remember, customer centricity is a continuous journey, not a destination.

CHAPTER 29

Harnessing the Power of Social Media for Business Growth

In today's digital age, social media has become an indispensable tool for businesses to connect with customers, build brand awareness, and drive growth. In this chapter, we'll explore the benefits of social media for business, how to create a social media strategy, and tips for leveraging social media to achieve your business goals.

Benefits of Social Media for Business

- Increased brand awareness and reach
- Improved customer engagement and loyalty
- Enhanced customer insights and feedback
- Cost-effective marketing and advertising
- Real-time customer service and support

Creating a Social Media Strategy

- Define your target audience and goals
- Choose relevant social media platforms
- Develop a content calendar and content types
- Set metrics and KPIs for measurement
- Engage with customers and respond to feedback

Tips for Leveraging Social Media

- Be authentic and consistent in your brand voice
- Use visual content to capture attention

- Utilize influencer marketing and user-generated content
- Run social media contests and giveaways
- Monitor and analyze your performance data

Conclusion

Social media has transformed the way businesses interact with customers and build their brand. By harnessing the power of social media, entrepreneurs can tap into new markets, foster customer loyalty, and drive business growth. Remember, social media is a constantly evolving landscape, so stay adaptable and innovative in your approach.

CHAPTER 30
Creating a Sustainable Supply Chain

In today's global economy, supply chains are critical to business success. However, traditional supply chain practices can have a significant impact on the environment and society. In this chapter, we'll explore the importance of sustainability in supply chain management, how to create a sustainable supply chain, and strategies for reducing environmental and social impact.

Why Sustainability in Supply Chain Matters

- Reduces carbon footprint and environmental impact
- Improves social responsibility and ethical practices
- Enhances brand reputation and customer loyalty
- Increases efficiency and cost savings
- Ensures long-term viability and risk management

Creating a Sustainable Supply Chain

- Conduct a supply chain assessment and set goals
- Implement sustainable sourcing and procurement practices
- Optimize logistics and transportation for reduced emissions
- Develop closed-loop and circular economy strategies
- Engage and collaborate with suppliers and stakeholders

Strategies for Reducing Environmental and Social Impact

- Implement green packaging and waste reduction initiatives
- Incorporate renewable energy and carbon offsetting

- Promote fair labor practices and ethical sourcing
- Develop diversity and inclusion programs for suppliers
- Invest in emerging technologies for supply chain innovation

Conclusion

Creating a sustainable supply chain is essential for businesses that want to reduce their environmental and social impact while improving their bottom line. By integrating sustainability into supply chain management, entrepreneurs can create a competitive advantage, enhance their brand reputation, and contribute to a more sustainable future. Remember, sustainability is a continuous journey that requires ongoing commitment and innovation.

CHAPTER 31
Scaling Your Business: Strategies and Challenges

As your business grows, you'll face new challenges and opportunities. Scaling your business requires careful planning, strategic decision-making, and a deep understanding of your market, customers, and operations. In this chapter, we'll explore the strategies and challenges of scaling your business, from expanding your team and processes to managing finances and maintaining your brand's integrity.

Strategies for Scaling Your Business

- Develop a scalable business model and growth strategy
- Build a strong, agile leadership team and organizational structure
- Continuously innovate and improve products and services
- Expand customer acquisition and retention strategies
- Optimize operations and processes for efficiency and productivity
- Manage finances and cash flow effectively

Challenges of Scaling Your Business

- Maintaining brand consistency and quality
- Managing cultural and organizational changes
- Balancing growth with financial and operational sustainability
- Adapting to changing market trends and customer needs

- Ensuring effective communication and collaboration across teams
- Mitigating risks and navigating regulatory complexities

Conclusion

Scaling your business is a complex and exciting journey that requires careful planning, execution, and continuous improvement. By understanding the strategies and challenges of scaling, entrepreneurs can position their businesses for long-term success, maintain their brand's integrity, and achieve their growth goals. Remember, scaling is a journey, not a destination, and requires ongoing adaptation and innovation.

CHAPTER 32
The Role of Technology in Entrepreneurship

In today's digital age, technology plays a vital role in entrepreneurship. It has leveled the playing field, providing access to tools, resources, and customers that were previously out of reach. In this chapter, we'll explore the impact of technology on entrepreneurship, the benefits and challenges of tech adoption, and strategies for leveraging technology to grow your business.

The Impact of Technology on Entrepreneurship

*   Democratized access to resources and customers
*   Increased efficiency and productivity
*   Enhanced collaboration and communication
*   New business models and revenue streams
*   Global reach and scalability

Benefits of Technology Adoption

*   Automation and streamlining of processes
*   Data-driven decision-making
*   Improved customer engagement and experience
*   Increased competitiveness and innovation
*   Access to new markets and customers

Challenges of Technology Adoption

*   Initial investment and costs
*   Technical expertise and talent acquisition

- Cybersecurity and data privacy concerns
- Constant evolution and staying up-to-date
- Balancing tech with human touch

Strategies for Leveraging Technology

- Identify and prioritize areas for tech integration
- Develop a technology roadmap and budget
- Build a team with diverse tech skills and expertise
- Embrace cloud computing and software-as-a-service
- Continuously evaluate and optimize tech solutions

Conclusion

Technology has transformed the landscape of entrepreneurship, offering unprecedented opportunities for innovation, growth, and impact. By understanding the role of technology in entrepreneurship and leveraging it strategically, entrepreneurs can gain a competitive edge, enhance their operations, and create new possibilities for their businesses and customers alike. Remember, technology is a means to an end, not an end in itself, and should be aligned with your business goals and values.

CHAPTER 33

The Importance of Data-Driven Decision Making

In today's business landscape, data has become a vital asset for entrepreneurs. Data-driven decision making enables entrepreneurs to make informed, strategic choices that drive growth, innovation, and profitability. In this chapter, we'll explore the importance of data-driven decision making, how to implement a data-driven approach, and best practices for leveraging data to drive business success.

Why Data-Driven Decision-Making Matters

- Improves decision-making accuracy and confidence
- Enhances operational efficiency and productivity
- Identifies new business opportunities and revenue streams
- Optimizes customer experiences and engagement
- Encourages a culture of continuous improvement

Implementing a Data-Driven Approach

- Define key performance indicators (KPIs) and metrics
- Collect, integrate, and analyze data from various sources
- Develop data visualization and reporting tools
- Foster a data-driven culture and mindset
- Continuously evaluate and refine data processes

Best Practices for Leveraging Data

- Use data to validate assumptions and hypotheses
- Conduct A/B testing and experiments to inform decisions
- Monitor and analyze customer behavior and feedback
- Track and optimize key metrics and KPIs
- Leverage predictive analytics and machine learning

Conclusion

Data-driven decision making is a critical component of successful entrepreneurship. By leveraging data, entrepreneurs can make informed decisions, optimize operations, and drive growth. Remember, data is a tool, not a replacement for human judgment, and should be used to augment and support business decisions, not dictate them

CHAPTER 34

Social Responsibility and Ethics in Entrepreneurship

As entrepreneurs, we have a responsibility to create businesses that not only generate profits but also positively impact society and the environment. In this chapter, we'll explore the importance of social responsibility and ethics in entrepreneurship, how to integrate these values into your business, and best practices for sustainable and responsible entrepreneurship.

Why Social Responsibility and Ethics Matter

- Builds trust and credibility with customers and stakeholders
- Attracts top talent and improves employee engagement
- Enhances brand reputation and differentiates your business
- Contributes to a better world and mitigates negative impacts
- Encourages long-term thinking and sustainability

Integrating Social Responsibility and Ethics into Your Business

- Define your values and mission statement
- Conduct a social and environmental impact assessment
- Develop policies and practices that promote responsibility and ethics
- Engage with stakeholders and report on progress
- Continuously evaluate and improve your social and environmental impact

Best Practices for Sustainable and Responsible Entrepreneurship

- Embed social and environmental considerations into your business model
- Measure and report on your triple bottom line (TBL) performance
- Incorporate circular economy principles into your operations
- Engage in transparent and ethical supply chain management
- Advocate for policies and practices that support a sustainable future

Conclusion

Social responsibility and ethics are essential components of entrepreneurship, enabling businesses to create long-term value for both shareholders and society. By integrating these values into your business, you'll not only contribute to a better world but also build a strong reputation, attract top talent, and drive sustainable growth. Remember, entrepreneurship is about creating value beyond just profits; it's about leaving a positive impact on the world.

CHAPTER 35

Overcoming Common Startup Challenges

Starting a business is a thrilling adventure, but it's also fraught with challenges that can make or break your venture. In this chapter, we'll explore some of the most common startup challenges and provide practical advice on how to overcome them.

Common Startup Challenges

- Developing a scalable business model
- Securing funding and managing cash flow
- Building and managing a team
- Defining and targeting a market segment
- Dealing with regulatory and legal hurdles
- Managing stress and maintaining work-life balance

Strategies for Overcoming Startup Challenges

- Develop a clear and adaptable business plan
- Build a strong network of mentors, advisors, and peers
- Prioritize cash flow management and diversify funding sources
- Focus on employee development and culture building
- Stay lean and agile, and pivot when necessary
- Practice self-care and prioritize mental health

Conclusion

Starting a business is never easy, but with the right mindset and strategies, you can overcome common startup challenges and build a successful and sustainable venture. Remember, resilience and adaptability are key to navigating the ups and downs of entrepreneurship. By understanding the challenges that lie ahead and developing strategies to overcome them, you'll be better equipped to succeed in the fast-paced and ever-changing world of startups.

CHAPTER 36

Title: Building a Resilient and Adaptable Organization

In the competitive world of entrepreneurship, success is often determined by an organization's ability to weather storms, adapt to change, and emerge stronger from challenges. Building a resilient and adaptable organization is not only essential for survival but also for sustainable growth and long-term viability. This chapter delves into the intricacies of fostering resilience and adaptability within an organization, offering practical insights, strategies, and real-world examples to inspire and guide entrepreneurs on their journey.

Understanding Resilience and Adaptability

Resilience and adaptability are two fundamental pillars that form the bedrock of a successful organization. Resilience refers to the capacity to bounce back from setbacks, navigate adversity, and emerge stronger. It encompasses the ability to withstand external pressures, pivot in response to changing circumstances, and maintain operational stability amid turbulence. Adaptability, on the other hand, involves the agility and flexibility to embrace change, innovate, and capitalize on new opportunities. Together, resilience and adaptability equip an organization to thrive in dynamic and unpredictable environments, positioning it for sustainable success.

Creating a Culture of Resilience

At the heart of building a resilient and adaptable organization lies the cultivation of a culture that champions these qualities. Leaders play a pivotal role in setting the tone and fostering a resilient mindset among their teams. By promoting open communication, transparency, and a growth-oriented outlook, leaders can instill confidence and fortitude within the organization. Embracing failure as a learning opportunity, nurturing a supportive work environment, and celebrating resilience in the face of challenges are key elements in shaping a resilient culture.

Strategies for Enhancing Organizational Resilience

Effective strategies are indispensable in fortifying organizational resilience. Diversifying revenue streams, proactively managing risks, and fostering strong relationships with stakeholders can bolster a company's ability to navigate uncertainties. Moreover, investing in robust infrastructure, leveraging technology for agility, and cultivating a responsive supply chain are essential components of resilience-building efforts. Organizations should also prioritize talent development, empowering employees with the skills and mindset needed to adapt and thrive amidst change.

Embracing Change and Innovation

Adaptability hinges on an organization's capacity to embrace change and drive innovation. By fostering a culture of continuous improvement and experimentation, entrepreneurs can ignite a spirit of innovation within their organizations. Encouraging cross-functional collaboration, soliciting diverse perspectives, and remaining attuned to market shifts enable organizations to proactively adapt to evolving conditions. Embracing technological advancements and staying abreast of industry trends position organizations to seize new opportunities and stay ahead of the curve.

Realizing the Benefits of Resilience and Adaptability

Organizations that prioritize resilience and adaptability stand to gain a multitude of benefits. Beyond weathering immediate challenges, they are better equipped to capitalize on emerging trends, outmaneuver competitors, and sustain growth over the long term. Moreover, fostering a resilient and adaptable culture fosters employee engagement, strengthens stakeholder confidence, and enhances the organization's reputation.

Embracing the Journey of Building Resilient and Adaptable Organizations

Building a resilient and adaptable organization is an ongoing journey rather than a destination. It requires continuous vigilance, strategic foresight, and a steadfast commitment to cultivating a culture of resilience and adaptability. As entrepreneurs embark on this transformative endeavor, they are poised to transform challenges into opportunities, propel their organizations to new heights, and leave an indelible mark on the entrepreneurial landscape.

In crafting a resilient and adaptable organization, entrepreneurs are charting a course for sustained success, forging a legacy that transcends transient triumphs and setbacks. By embracing the principles and practices delineated in this chapter, entrepreneurs can fortify their organizations, elevate their teams, and navigate the dynamic terrain of entrepreneurship with unwavering resilience and unwavering adaptability.

CHAPTER 37

The Art of Leadership in a Startup Environment

Starting a business requires more than just a great idea - it requires strong leadership to guide the team towards success. In this chapter, we will explore the unique challenges of leadership in a startup environment and provide practical strategies for entrepreneurs to lead their teams effectively.

The Unique Challenges of Leadership in a Startup Environment

- Managing limited resources and tight deadlines
- Building and motivating a small team
- Navigating uncertainty and constant change
- Balancing short-term needs with long-term goals

Effective Leadership Strategies for Entrepreneurs

- Developing a clear and compelling vision
- Leading by example and embodying company values
- Fostering open communication and feedback
- Empowering team members to take ownership and make decisions
- Prioritizing employee development and growth
- Building a strong company culture
- Staying adaptable and agile in a rapidly changing environment

Conclusion

Leadership is a critical component of startup success, and entrepreneurs must develop the skills and strategies necessary to lead their teams effectively. By fostering a strong culture, empowering team members, and prioritizing employee development, entrepreneurs can position their startups for success and create a lasting impact.

CHAPTER 38

Raising Capital and Managing Investments

Raising capital and managing investments are crucial components of building a successful startup. In this chapter, we will explore the various ways to raise capital, manage investments, and create a successful investment strategy.

Raising Capital

- Understanding the different types of investors (venture capital, angel investors, crowdfunding)
- Preparing a persuasive pitch and business plan
- Building a strong financial model and projections
- Negotiating terms and closing the deal
- Understanding the importance of due diligence
- Preparing for potential pitfalls and setbacks

Managing Investments

- Understanding the importance of cash flow management
- Creating a diversified investment portfolio
- Managing risk and measuring performance
- Building strategic partnerships with investors
- Understanding the role of board members and advisors
- Navigating the challenges of scaling and exiting

Conclusion

Raising capital and managing investments require careful planning, strategic decision-making, and effective communication. By understanding the different types of investors, preparing a strong pitch and financial model, and building a diversified investment portfolio, entrepreneurs can create a successful investment strategy that fuels growth and drives success. With the right approach, entrepreneurs can navigate the challenges of raising capital and managing investments and build a strong foundation for their startup's future.

CHAPTER 39

Exit Strategies for Entrepreneurs

As an entrepreneur, you've invested countless hours, resources, and energy into building your business. But eventually, you'll need to exit your company. Whether you're looking to retire, pursue new opportunities, or simply cash out, a well-planned exit strategy is essential. In this book, we'll explore various exit strategies, helping you maximize your returns and ensure a smooth transition.

Mergers and Acquisitions (M&As)

* Understanding the M&A process
* Finding potential buyers
* Negotiating the deal

Initial Public Offerings (IPOs)

* Advantages and disadvantages of going public
* Preparing for an IPO
* Navigating the IPO process

Private Equity and Venture Capital Exit

* Understanding private equity and venture capital firms
* Preparing for a private equity or venture capital exit
* Maximizing value in a private equity or venture capital deal

Strategic Acquisitions

* Identifying potential strategic buyers
* Building relationships with strategic acquirers
* Negotiating a strategic acquisition

Management Buyouts (MBOs)

* Understanding MBOs and their benefits
* Planning and executing an MBO
* Financing options for MBOs

Family Succession and Estate Planning

* Transferring ownership to the next generation
* Estate planning and tax implications
* Ensuring a smooth transition

Liquidation and Wind-Down

* Understanding the liquidation process
* Preparing for a wind-down
* Maximizing value in a liquidation scenario

Conclusion

Choosing the right exit strategy is crucial for entrepreneurs, as it can significantly impact their financial returns and legacy. By understanding the various options and planning ahead, entrepreneurs can ensure a smooth transition and achieve their goals. Whether you're looking to exit soon or in the future, this book has provided you with the essential knowledge to make informed decisions and navigate the exit process with confidence.

CHAPTER 40

Reflections on Success: Lessons Learned from Seasoned Entrepreneurs

As a entrepreneur, you are constantly striving to build a successful business, create a legacy, and make a meaningful impact. But what does it really take to achieve success? In this book, we'll explore the lessons learned from seasoned entrepreneurs who have walked the path and achieved remarkable success. We'll delve into their stories, experiences, and insights, uncovering the key takeaways that can guide you on your own journey to success.

Embrace Failure, Learn from Mistakes

*   Overcoming fear of failure
*   How failure can lead to growth and resilience
*   The importance of reflecting on mistakes

Build a Strong Network, Build a Strong Business

*   The power of mentorship and networking
*   Nurturing relationships with peers and mentors
*   Leveraging connections for growth and support

Passion, Purpose, and Perseverance

*   Discovering your why and staying true to your vision
*   Cultivating passion and purpose in your work
*   Persevering through challenges and setbacks

Adapt and Evolve, Stay Ahead of the Game

*   Embracing change and staying agile
*   Continuously learning and innovating
*   Anticipating market shifts and capitalizing on opportunities

Build a Strong Team, Build a Strong Business

*   The importance of hiring for culture and skills
*   Empowering and developing your team
*   Fostering a culture of collaboration and trust

Stay Humble, Stay Hungry

*   The dangers of complacency and ego
*   Remaining humble and open to feedback
*   Continuously seeking knowledge and growth

Conclusion

Success is a journey, not a destination. The lessons learned from seasoned entrepreneurs remind us that failure is a teacher, relationships are key, passion and purpose fuel our work, adaptability is crucial, strong teams are essential, and humility is vital. Embrace these principles and let them guide you on your own path to success. Remember, success is not just about achieving goals, but also about the person you become in the process.

About the Author:
Raymond M. Penny

Raymond M. Penny is a visionary entrepreneur, prolific author, and influential figure in the realm of business and innovation. With a steadfast commitment to reshaping the landscape of entrepreneurship, Raymond has ignited a trailblazing legacy driven by his unwavering passion for creating transformative impact.

As the founder of RMP Mobile Notary and Immigration Services, Raymond has revolutionized the notary and immigration services industry, spearheading an enterprise that prioritizes accessibility, efficiency, and unwavering dedication to client satisfaction. His entrepreneurial spirit and innovative approach have positioned RMP Mobile Notary and Immigration Services as a cornerstone of reliability and excellence within its domain.

In addition to his entrepreneurial endeavors, Raymond has established himself as a sought-after author and ghostwriter, leveraging his profound expertise and insightful perspective to inspire and guide aspiring entrepreneurs and business leaders. His compelling writings exemplify a fusion of profound wisdom, practical strategies, and empathetic guidance, offering a beacon of enlightenment for individuals navigating the intricate pathways of entrepreneurship and business ownership.

Throughout his illustrious career, Raymond has embodied the ethos of innovation, resilience, and unwavering determination, solidifying his reputation as a dynamic force within the entrepreneurial community. His multifaceted accomplishments reflect an unyielding commitment to fostering growth, empowering others, and catalyzing meaningful change in the ever-evolving landscape of business.

Raymond's journey stands as a testament to the transformative power of entrepreneurship, serving as a source of inspiration for countless individuals who dare to dream, innovate, and redefine the boundaries of success. With an indomitable spirit and an unwavering pursuit of excellence, Raymond continues to leave an indelible mark on the world, embodying the very essence of visionary leadership and entrepreneurial acumen.

As we delve into the profound insights and invaluable wisdom offered by Raymond M. Penny, we are invited to embark on a transformative odyssey, where every page unfolds a new dimension of entrepreneurial enlightenment and emboldens us to embrace the boundless potential that lies within our reach.